DATE DUE

GAYLORD			PRINTED IN U.S.A.

D0349603

Behind Media

Advertising

Catherine Chambers

HEINEMANN
LIBRARY

www.heinemann.co.uk/library
Visit our website to find out more information about **Heinemann Library** books.

To order:
☎ Phone 44 (0) 1865 888066
📄 Send a fax to 44 (0) 1865 314091
💻 Visit the Heinemann Bookshop at www.heinemann.co.uk/library to browse our catalogue and order online.

First published in Great Britain by Heinemann Library, Halley Court, Jordan Hill, Oxford, OX2 8EJ,
a division of Reed Educational and Professional Publishing Ltd.
Heinemann is a registered trademark of Reed Educational and Professional Publishing Ltd.

OXFORD MELBOURNE AUCKLAND
JOHANNESBURG BLANTYRE GABORONE
IBADAN PORTSMOUTH NH (USA) CHICAGO

© Reed Educational and Professional Publishing Ltd 2001
The moral right of the proprietor has been asserted.

All rights reserved. No part of this publication may be reproduced, stored in a retrieval system, or transmitted in
any form or by any means, electronic, mechanical, photocopying, recording, or otherwise without either the prior
written permission of the publishers or a licence permitting restricted copying in the United Kingdom issued by the
Copyright Licensing Agency Ltd, 90 Tottenham Court Road, London W1P 0LP.

Designed by Paul Davies and Associates
Originated by Ambassador Litho Ltd.
Printed in Hong Kong/China

ISBN 0 431 11450 1
05 04 03 02 01
10 9 8 7 6 5 4 3 2 1

British Library Cataloguing in Publication Data

Chambers, Catherine
   Advertising. - (Behind Media)
   1.Advertising - Juvenile literature
   I.Title
   659.1

Acknowledgements
The Publishers would like to thank the following for permission to reproduce photographs:
Arena Images: p30, Colin Willoughby p37; Benneton: p43; Cadbury's: p23; Corbis: p13, Kevin Fleming p27, Lyn
Hughes p41, Rob Rowan p22; De Beers: p45; Greg Evans: pp8, 10, 14; John P. Johnson: p32; Levi: pp21, 35;
Moviestore: pp33, 38; Oxfam: p28; Panos/Chris Johnson: p11; Robert Harding: p25, Simon Harris p4, Nigel Blythe
p5; Sainsbury's: p9; Stock Market: Rob Lewine p19, David Raymer p29, George Shelley p40; Stockbyte: p44;
Stone/Bruce Ayres: p6; Telegraph: Ron Chapple p39, Stephen Simpson p20; View: pp7, 15, 18;
Vin Mag Archive: p24.

Cover photograph reproduced with permission of Corbis.

Our thanks to Roger Thomas for his comments in the preparation of this book.

Every effort has been made to contact copyright holders of any material reproduced in this book.
Any omissions will be rectified in subsequent printings if notice is given to the publishers.

Contents

Any words appearing in the text in bold, **like this**, are explained in the Glossary.

Why Advertise?

Introduction

This Hong Kong tram takes its advertisement wherever it goes, reaching a wide range of people. It is beneficial for the advertiser, and helpful to the tram company, who gets paid for displaying someone else's goods or services.

More than 2000 years ago, advertisements for hotels and restaurants were displayed on the walls of Roman cities to entice passing merchants to stay in the city – and to spend. Outdoor advertising increased over the centuries and was the principle medium until about 400 years ago. Then, newspapers came on the scene and the idea of mass advertising began. Since then, every product and service imaginable has been promoted, capturing our attention and encouraging us to part with our money. Governments and local authorities, too, have used advertising to advise and inform us. This book explores the motives, methods and roles of advertisers. Specifically, it looks at how a jeans' manufacturer might put together its own advertising campaign.

What's the point?

Whether promoting a new product or reminding us of the benefits of an old one, advertising tries first to attract our attention, and then to persuade us that we need the product. We shall be looking at how companies work out the benefits of advertising, and the types of people they target. Billions of pounds are spent worldwide every year on advertising. Is it worth it?

We shall also take a look at why companies part with money for advertising and who pays for it in the end. Is advertising right? This book also explores the issues surrounding advertising and whether or not certain types of persuasion are **ethical**.

What's the best way?

Advertising and promotion is all around us – on the clothes we wear, the bags we carry, on the huge **hoardings** that colour our streets, on public transport, television, radio, in the newspapers and other media. We shall explore different advertising media and methods, and how a jeans' manufacturer might use them to promote a new **line**. The book also shows how a campaign might co-ordinate the use of different media through using the same colour, storyline and other devices.

Who makes it happen?

The world of advertising involves a wide range of jobs, from designing customer surveys to directing film **commercials**. We shall be looking at the roles of different personnel and the skills that they require to perform their tasks. We shall also be finding out the differences between publicity departments within companies, and advertising agencies.

What's next?

It might appear that methods of advertising have been exhausted. But we shall see that new technology is enabling us to choose which advertisements we wish to see at the press of a button – and at an ever-increasing speed. We can learn about what we want to buy and then pay for it without moving from our seat.

Tokyo's dazzling display of neon lights advertises the city itself as much as each individual product. It adds to the excitement of the night and encourages people to stay out later, buying goods or watching shows.

What's the point?

For a company providing goods or services, the aim of commercial advertising is to attract more customers. From the consumers' standpoint, it reminds them of what is available, and highlights the benefits of buying one particular product over another, and is often a form of entertainment in its own right. A jeans' manufacturer might be hoping to persuade young people to buy a new style of this traditional product.

Aiming to gain

Commercial advertising is largely about money and reputation – persuading people to take an interest in and buy a product because it is good. Products can range from manufactured goods to holiday destinations, or services such as banking and insurance. Advertising operates at two levels. The first is to increase sales without negative attractions, such as price-slashing, which will only yield a short-term benefit. The second is to increase a company's **market share** for their product. The latter is probably the most difficult to achieve. It is very easy in a jeans' campaign, for instance, just to promote jeans as a whole, not a particular **brand** or **line**. So the task for the advertiser is to persuade people of the uniqueness of its own product – maximising its strengths and highlighting its edge over others. To succeed, most companies and advertisers will want to both retain loyal customers of the brand and attract new ones. As traditional and new customers are often separate target groups with different tastes, this can be an almost impossible task!

People are queueing at the bank of their choice. Financial advertising is big business. The rapidly increasing number and range of banks is making competition very fierce, so advertising in this sector has boomed in recent years.

Getting to you!

But advertising is deeper and more subtle than just grabbing attention for a product. It tries to manipulate consumers' tastes so that they feel they are following the right trend by buying a particular product or service. It attempts, too, to alter the perceptions people have of themselves, making them think that they belong to a certain, special category of person. In these ways, consumers are led to believe that they deserve to own particular possessions or receive certain services. In other words, it helps them to justify parting with their money – and to feel good about themselves for possessing or using the product.

Advertising is also used to counter negative publicity – in other words to fix a problem with a product or service. In 2000, thousands of Ford cars were recalled because of fears about dangerous tyres. The tyres themselves were made by Firestone, not by Ford, but both manufacturers still have to rebuild confidence in the buyer through positive advertising campaigns.

The feel-good factor

Government advertising encourages its citizens to feel good about moulding their behaviour in order to avoid injury, death and damage to property. It also reminds us to pay our taxes! Charity advertising is very similar to commercial advertising. People are persuaded that by giving to charities they will be altering the balance of privileged and underprivileged people in the world. In other words, charity advertising appeals to the feel-good factor, just as any other type of advertising.

Stores such as this Arnott's department store in Dublin, Eire build lifestyle themes which they hope their customers will want for themselves. New ideas for fashion, home furnishings and decoration are often reinforced by television programmes using similar products and by 'product placement' in films.

Branding an image

Branding gives a range of products a distinctive image, often through its looks – maybe the design features, materials it uses, or the colours. People often associate a particular brand with a level of quality, or a certain feeling, such as comfort or excitement.

Advertising or publicity?

Advertising is a form of communication which aims to convey a specific set of messages about a product to as many people as possible. It is a targeted, integrated **campaign** over a specific length of time that might use different types of media to advertise goods and services. Publicity and promotion also try to attract attention for a product, but in a less structured way, targeting people more at random.

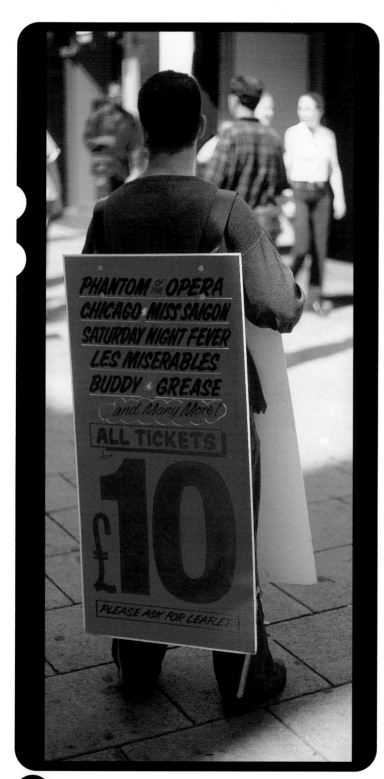

Many methods

Jeans' manufacturers include expensive designer labels which are sold all over the world, and cheaper, regionally or nationally distributed garments. In line with this, a jeans' advertising strategy can range from cheap publicity to huge international, multimedia advertising campaigns. Generally, the more the buyer pays for the **brand**, or make, the bigger and more sophisticated the advertising campaign. But the manufacturer still has to find something special to say about their product.

In recent years, jeans have been worn a lot by older people, which have given them an untrendy, negative image among the young. Random publicity methods on their own are probably not good enough to counter this. These methods include **direct mailing** to households, flyers, telephone sales and publicity stunts such as hot-air balloons stamped with the product logo. All are good ways of getting the consumer's attention. One of the simplest, cheapest and most effective forms of publicity is the logo, used to good effect in the clothes industry. This is usually the manufacturer's brand name embroidered on the garment itself. The beauty of it is that wherever the wearer goes, the logo goes, too. But all these are short-term measures. Advertising goes deeper, trying to create a desire for the product by providing a link between the consumers' tastes and the product's benefits.

Sandwich boards are a great way of advertising a show. Here in London, shoppers are being encouraged to buy cut-price tickets for a West End musical. A casual labour force is usually employed to wear the boards.

A new image

The international store, Marks and Spencer, has suffered a negative image in recent years. Like jeans, its clothes were perceived as old-fashioned and dull. But the store did not panic with a string of publicity stunts. Instead, for its UK market, the company spent the year from 1999 to 2000 researching women's sizes and found that the average woman has increased to a size 16, is 1 metre 62 centimetres (5 feet four inches) tall and wears a size 6 shoe. The advertising campaign that followed aimed at attracting more women by using size 16 models in various media.

Supermarkets often promote a product, such as this Port Salut cheese, by offering attractively presented samples near the store's entrance. As well as encouraging people to buy the cheese itself, promoters give ideas about what other foods or drinks could go with it, encouraging customers to buy more in the store.

The big issue

Sales promotions are a good way of attracting attention for a product. They include heavy discounts, offers of two-for-the price of one, free gifts if the purchaser buys within a certain time, and other incentives. However, in Germany, retailers are not allowed to use these methods because it is believed they can mislead the consumer about the real price and qualities of the product.

Around the world

Advertising is accessible to almost everyone and is created by large companies and **sole traders** in all countries. Even in the most remote mountain village, satellite communications enable people to receive **commercials** at least through radio, and often via television and the Internet. Huge multinational companies take advantage of these media all over the world.

Ads by all

Many advertisements in different countries reflect the spending power and the kinds of goods purchased by the majority of people living there. In economically developing countries, most advertisements are for cheap necessities, such as food and clothing, with only a small percentage promoting luxury goods such as cars and computers. In these countries, sole traders offer most of the available products. They create their own advertisements, which, though cheaply made, often include many of the sophisticated elements of much more expensive advertising, such as humour.

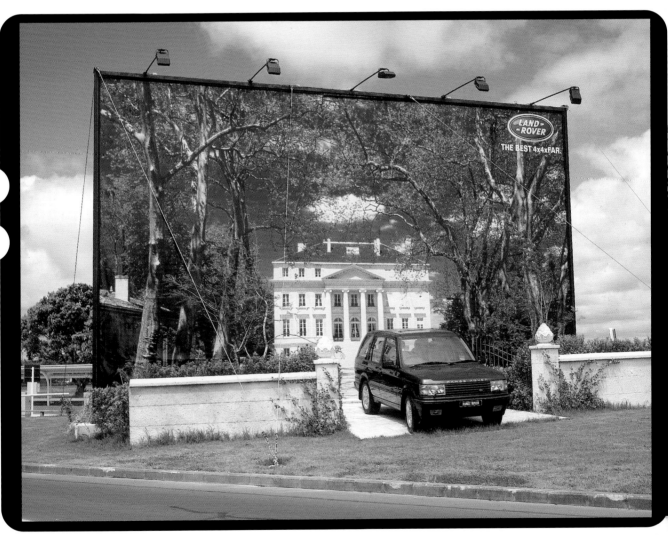

This type of advertisement is rarely seen outside rich nations, although it could be found on the Internet anywhere in the world. This new accessibility has created an increasing desire for luxury goods in communist countries such as China, where such items have previously been restricted.

Ads for all

Mass advertising, using a structured **campaign**, stemmed from the development of mass-production and improved printing processes in the 19th century, especially in the USA. Having saturated its own market with goods, the US then sought markets worldwide. As a result, its companies began to create advertising that was acceptable to people in different countries. With worldwide communications, advertising has become even more globalized.

Even the biggest brands, such as Coca-Cola, need to attract new markets for their products. This is in the face of **market saturation** in their traditional consumer countries, and increased competition from locally-produced supermarket brands of cola. But their campaigns do not work everywhere. Since the early 1990s, Coca-Cola has tried to break into the soft drinks industry in India, which has over a billion citizens – a massive market to be tapped into. But by 2000 they were still struggling after over six years of public protests outside their Indian headquarters. The protestors have included politicians, who believe that multinational companies, such as Coca-Cola, are spoiling India's local soft drinks' industry.

Here in Zimbabwe, a cold water washing powder is being advertised in English. Cold water cleaning seems attractive in countries where heating water can be difficult.

Unacceptable exploitation

International **brands** often advertise luxury goods in developing countries. These nations' governments and aid agencies have criticized some companies for promoting goods unnecessarily. One of these products is baby milk powder; another is toothpaste. In most parts of Africa, for instance, the proper use of chewing sticks makes toothpaste an expensive, unnecessary luxury for people who cannot afford it.

Getting it off the Ground

Is it worth it?

Studies by marketing organizations have proved that it is worth spending time and money on advertising, but only if a company advertises regularly and continually reviews its advertising strategy. For a jeans' company with a known **brand**, it would definitely be worth spending money on advertising a new style or **line** in the product range.

How do we know?

Economic organizations such as the UK's Strategic Planning Institute, advertising agencies and media owners, gather information from hundreds of different companies to assess the impact of advertising. Some of these companies have a strong commitment to advertising, Others only advertise when they want to promote a particular product, or when it looks as if the company is in financial trouble! Economic organizations in particular are respected for their verdicts on the benefits of advertising. How do they assess its impact?

The amount of money spent on advertising by companies producing the same kinds of goods is compared by the economic organizations. From these studies it shows that companies spending a lot on advertising usually get back more money from their efforts and **investment** than companies that do not. In other words, the advertising is so successful that it helps pay for itself. This is known as **return on investment**. Also compared is the average **market share** for similar products that are well advertised, and those that are not. Again, it has been found that if a company spends a lot on advertising, it will increase its share of the market for the advertised product, and possibly for other products in its range.

Was it successful?

It is easy to find out the benefits of some types of advertising, such as mail-order catalogues, where direct links can be made between advertising and selling. It is a more complex task to find out if, and how, other types of advertising have been successful. Some of the money set aside for advertising has to be spent on assessing the effectiveness of the **campaign** once it has ended, through **market research** techniques.

Counting the cost

The costs of advertising include market research, producing the advertisements, and buying advertising space in the various media, such as television, radio, newspapers, flyers and on **hoardings**. Some of the money goes on advertising personnel within a company, or on hiring an advertising agency.

Weighing it up

It is more difficult to sell some products and services without advertising than others. The difficulty can depend on the size and spread of the company's **client base** – the people who could use the product, and the competition for it. Companies that make goods for well-known brand names cannot fix their own label or logo onto their merchandise. This makes advertising their work very difficult, so they have to publicize it through **trade fairs** and the industry's catalogues, which the public do not see.

It is cheaper to advertise a product made by one company together with a different one made by another. For instance, a new line in jeans could team up with a new type of washing powder. But the aims of the two companies' campaigns would have to be similar for this marketing strategy to work. Their targeted client base would have to be the same. In our imaginary jeans' campaign, the new line in jeans will be more appropriately advertised together with a mobile phone company. Both will be targeting a young client base.

Who pays?

All advertising costs have to be paid for. Many customers are suspicious that the advertising budget is added to the cost of the product rather than being taken out of the producer's profits. If advertising leads to a lot of profits, producers claim that the cost of the product can be reduced in the future. But does this often happen?

*The window is an important advertising space for a shop, and is redressed regularly. Advertisers try to change their adverts and **commercials** to keep the public interested.*

What do they want?

Even before a product has been designed, a company producing a new **line** of jeans would want to know the likes and dislikes of its target market. Once the jeans have been designed, it needs to find out if the target market approves of them. To do this, companies do some **market research**.

What's the target?

For jeans, an obvious market opportunity in recent years has been young people. This is because the product has an unfashionable image with some members of this group. The company that can win back this market will make a fortune! First, market researchers ask the target group about their tastes and lifestyles, using a specific set of questions and a variety of techniques such as telephone or postal questionnaires, face-to-face questioning in shopping centres or door-to-door interviewing, targeting areas where particular social groups live.

Market researchers on the streets have to make sure that they do not keep the person being questioned from getting on with their shopping, or going back to work. This makes the public rushed and irritated. Their answers will not be carefully thought out.

Another technique is the **focus group** – a gathering of people with similar lifestyles, who are often asked more detailed questions by the market researcher than questionnaires allow. People are often targeted according to their job. **Marketing managers** develop an idea of the kind of lifestyle and needs of each group of people so they can target their product more accurately. As well as other information, market research gives a company an idea of the attraction for a product on a demographic basis. This means they get to know where in the country their ideas are most or least popular.

On the job

A market researcher has to be very good with the public – friendly and respectful. But he or she also has to be gently persuasive to tease out the detailed reasons why someone likes or dislikes a product. A market researcher has to learn how to ask the right questions without giving away their own opinion.

Pester power

Pester power is the advertising industry's name for the influence that young people have on their parents' buying habits. This power is a huge factor in selling many products, from computer games and videos to trainers – and jeans. Although young people are sometimes targeted by market researchers on the street, much of the work is done through focus groups. With young people, the market researcher first asks about general interests, likes and dislikes over a whole range of products and concepts such as colours, shapes, sports, food and so on. Then they move on to the specific product. The researcher will also ask young people what happens to them, and how they feel, if they do not have the latest product on the market.

Shop managers know a lot about the market for the products they sell. A marketing manager for the new line in jeans would benefit from asking them which ranges of jeans are popular among particular age or social groups.

Taking liberties

Market research conducted through postal questionnaires often asks very detailed questions about a person's family, financial situation and spending habits. Many people find this very intrusive and are not convinced that the information they give will be kept confidential. Many market research companies try to encourage people to fill in the questionnaires by offering a prize draw.

What's the plan?

This is the kind of communication network that would be used by a large company employing an advertising agency to create a campaign for a new product. For example, the Jeans' Company deals directly and only with the Account Executive at the Advertising Agency. He or she in turn communicates with the various Agency departments.

The **marketing manager** for a company has to create an advertising plan. This depends on the whole company's aims for their future, and the amount of money available to spend on the advertising **campaign**.

A question of scale

Small companies and **sole traders** often plan and execute their own advertising strategy. If they want to use the media, such as local radio or the press, they will ask the radio station's or newspaper's advertising section to put together advertisements, giving them an idea of the aims and the budget. But a larger company will probably have a marketing team of its own, which creates a full advertising plan. The marketing manager will then nearly always employ an advertising agency to develop specific ideas for advertisements. These will be produced for various media, such as newspapers, television and radio.

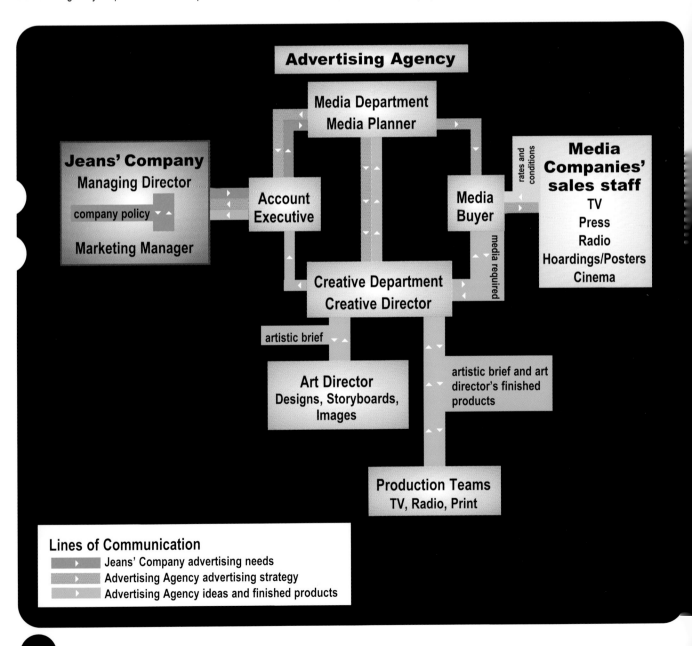

Advertising Agency

Media Department
Media Planner

Jeans' Company
Managing Director
company policy
Marketing Manager

Account Executive

Media Buyer

rates and conditions

media required

Media Companies' sales staff
TV
Press
Radio
Hoardings/Posters
Cinema

Creative Department
Creative Director

artistic brief

Art Director
Designs, Storyboards, Images

artistic brief and art director's finished products

Production Teams
TV, Radio, Print

Lines of Communication
Jeans' Company advertising needs
Advertising Agency advertising strategy
Advertising Agency ideas and finished products

On the job

A **marketing manager** organizes a company's advertising and promotion, including employing advertising agencies for high-profile campaigns. For an international **brand**, he or she needs to have a good knowledge of the cultural, economic and social make-up of a wide range of countries. The manager also has to be aware of successful advertising techniques across different media. He or she needs excellent personal relationship and negotiating skills.

Step by step

Before the advertising plan can be established, the marketing manager has to understand the company plan, which is developed by the company's managing director and key assistant managers. A good company plan shows where the company is now in terms of sales, income and development, where it wants to be in the near and far future, and how it thinks it can get there.

The marketing manager uses the company plan to make sure that the advertising plan fits with the short and long-term aims of the company. The marketing team will then be able to work out how much can be spent on advertising, what types of advertisement will be needed, and where they will be shown. The marketing manager can then confidently present the aims of both the advertising plan and the company to the advertising agency. This in turn helps the agency to prepare the pitch of its campaign – who it is targeting, where, and how. Knowledge speeds everything up, making the campaign more effective, and cheaper. Many agencies charge by the hour that each of its personnel work on a particular client's project, or **account**.

Knowing the product

The marketing manager must know the product really well, especially the unique features that will make it attractive to the target market. As well as this, he or she must know the competition, and how that competition advertises itself. Over the years, jeans' brands such as Lee Cooper and Levi have sometimes stressed the traditional nature of their product, to keep people confident in it. This particularly attracted older consumers. But Levi then tried to appeal to younger people by making their product seem sensual. This it achieved mainly through a series of TV **commercials** set in a laundrette, in which a Levi-wearer slowly stripped off their jeans. In 2000, Levi changed tack again – this time showing the flexible nature of their new jeans material and design. Again this was aimed at the young. Such a campaign will probably attract the youth market with its relaxed, versatile image.

Technical tips

An advertising plan needs to take into consideration four key points: the product itself, the price, the distribution of the product – where it is going – and marketing communications, which include advertising. These four aims are often known as the four 'p's – product, price, place and promotion. In addition, it is wise to add a 'c' – the competition that the product faces.

The marketing machine

It is a well-known saying among advertisers that 50 per cent of the time their work is ineffective. And if only they all knew which 50 per cent that was, everyone would save a lot of time and money! This hit-and-miss aspect makes some companies ignore advertising altogether, while others employ the best agency that they can to try and hit the target market.

Choosing the agency

A high-profile **campaign** for a new **line** in jeans would require the skills of a professional advertising agency. The company producing the jeans has to choose the agency carefully. To do this, their **marketing manager** studies the past results of advertising agencies they have used before, and those gathered through professional directories and by word of mouth. Each selected agency is then approached and given a package containing the details of the product and the target market. They are asked to present a brief advertising strategy, with rough ideas for the campaign sketched on **storyboards**. The agency with the best ideas, and the best attitude, is then selected. The jeans' marketing manager would ensure that there is a good relationship between the agency and the company.

Saatchi and Saatchi Compton is a huge international advertising agency with offices in Australia, the European continent, the UK and the USA. Their clients have even included political parties.

In their hands

The running of the jeans' campaign has now been transferred to the advertising agency. The company producing the jeans is now a client of the agency, and the job being done for it is known as its **account**. The jeans' marketing manager is kept informed of progress and the state of the budget through the agency's **account executive**. They meet to discuss the budget, the product's selling points, and the competition it faces. More **market research** will be undertaken by the agency, often using **focus groups** to see which storyboard ideas they find most attractive. With all the information gathered, work can begin.

Creative teams have to produce a selection of ideas for their clients. But there is nearly always one that the team has most faith in and enthusiasm for. Often this is the most bizarre idea, which can sometimes be difficult for the client to accept.

Down to work

The project is taken forward by the agency's media and creative departments. The media department is led by a **media planner**, who chooses and co-ordinates the different media through which the product is being advertised. In the creative department, the creative director heads brainstorming sessions with the art director, the head **copywriter** and their teams, until the right theme and look for the campaign is created. The client helps choose the final thrust of the campaign. The creative director then co-ordinates the work, making sure that it is completed on time. The designers then produce images, logos, storyboards and **layouts**, while the copywriters produce the words for the campaign, including scripts for **commercials**.

On the job

An account executive has to know about every aspect of producing an effective campaign, from budgeting to the creative process. He or she must be tactful with the client and the agency's teams, but firm in keeping the project on time and within budget. The executive has to bear in mind that a successful campaign for the client means equal success for the agency.

Getting the message

The **copywriter's** role in a multimedia **campaign** is to create **copy** – the written words of the campaign. This includes a **slogan** suitable for still and moving images, **endlines** for radio **commercials**, which reinforce the message and image of the product, and scripts for radio and TV commercials.

Setting the scene

For an expensive multimedia campaign, the creative team usually develops a storyline and setting, which is the basis for all still adverts and moving or spoken commercials. The storyline co-ordinates the campaign through image, colour, and, very importantly, words. Each product is unique, so the copywriter must treat it appropriately. The setting and copy for the imaginary jeans' campaign would be totally unsuitable for, say, an international aid agency or a stairlift for the elderly.

The jeans have been designed using a lighter, more flexible denim, and have a special, secure pocket for a mobile phone. The jeans' company is working with a mobile phone company on a joint advertising campaign, although the jeans' company has the lead role and a bigger **investment**. The copywriter might create a name for the jeans which combines the ideas of confidence and youth, such as 'dream jeanzzz', the 'zzz' sound indicating cool relaxation, but which in the radio and TV media can also be used as the sound of a mobile phone.

The copywriting and design teams have to work together closely to produce words and images that match each other and the mood and aims of the campaign. The slogan must trigger the memory of the audience when they hear or see it for the second time. In recent years, humour has been one of the copywriter's greatest assets.

Technical tips

In 2000, Levi jeans created the slogan 'Engineered jeans – twisted to fit'. The repetition of the 'j' sound in the first part of the slogan, and the 'ist' and 'it' part of the second is a very catchy technique and popular with copywriters. So, too, is rhyme, for example 'dream cream', and assonance, which is imperfect rhyme, such as 'dream jeanzzz'.

Slick slogans

The team has to create a storyline for the TV and film commercials, from which stills can be taken for **hoardings** and posters, and from which a slogan can be written. It might go something like this: two young people are tossed from the sky onto a deserted island beach. They both start dreaming of tempting food and thirst-quenching drinks. The one not wearing 'dream jeanzzz' searches frantically for food and water. The other, wearing the jeans, pulls out a mobile phone from the special pocket and orders sumptuous food and drink, which is then delivered by a helicopter. The copywriter might create the slogan – 'not just dreamzzz', which would be used for all media. For posters and hoardings, this would be the only copy.

LEVI'S® ENGINEERED JEANS™
TWISTED TO FIT

levi.com

On the job

A copywriter has to be able to create copy for every mood, from humorous to serious. He or she needs a knack for rhythm and punchiness, and the techniques explained in the technical tips box. The copywriter must make the copy reflect the image of the product, the company and the campaign. Catchiness and appropriate mood are essential.

It is clear that the image for the new Levi's jeans fits the slogan. The two people's legs are twisted around each other, wrapped up together.

Looking good

All creative personnel must bear in mind the two main aims of every campaign – the strengths of the product and the needs of the market. The design team has to make sure that these are successfully incorporated in all their **visuals** – **storyboards** for TV **commercials** and sketched **stills** for newspaper, poster and **hoarding** advertisements.

People appeal

The jeans' campaign is targeting the youth market. But a market is not looking at the advertisements – individual people are. So through the creative teams' brainstorming sessions, they have come up with an image and storyline which they hope will capture and keep the attention of each person, whether male or female. One of the commercial advantages of the product itself is that it is unisex. But this just makes the design team's work more complex! Some products, such as the Fiat Punto and Punta car range, have got round the problem by creating separate but complementary advertisements aimed at each gender.

Before photographers and TV commercial production teams can get to work, the designer will produce accurate **layouts** *for the stills and refined storyboards to show the creative director and the client. These are far more polished than the rough sketches first produced (see page 18).*

Setting the scene

For the fictitious jeans' campaign, each type of visual has to include both the jeans and the mobile phone, according to the storyline descibed on the previous pages. The designers would use the setting of the storyline, and the colours and mood that they have agreed on with their clients. In tune with this, and the desired relaxed, yet confident, image the design team might produce sketches in which a young model or actor looks sharp and cool in a dreamy beach setting. The jeans are traditional blue, but the background colours are white sands, pale pebbles, and grey-green grasses. The sun is hazy and hot and the sky blue with wispy clouds. This translates well to all visuals, whether moving or still.

Down to the detail

The designer's job includes choosing lettering for stills. He or she has to work out the size and style of **font** for the name of the jeans, and the **slogan**. It must be suitable for all media. The designer must always bear in mind the products being advertised and the chosen theme. So for the name, 'dream jeanzzz', and the slogan, the designer might, for instance, choose the square kind of lettering found on the visual display of a mobile phone. The poster and hoarding have only the slogan on them but the newspaper advertisement requires more, smaller lettering giving details about the product. This, too, must reflect the product's image.

Some products and companies rely on the recognition and popularity of their advertisements' traditional colour schemes and lettering that have been used for decades. Keeping these can give the public confidence in the product, believing that if advertising design has not changed, then neither has the company's standards.

Technical tips

The impact of a written slogan depends a lot on how it looks. A designer has a huge range of fonts, sizes and styles to choose from, many now available on computer word processing and design programs. The designer must make sure that the font stands out against any image behind it, so he or she might choose a jeans'-blue lettering against the silver-sand beach.

Followers of fashion

The creative team for a jeans' **campaign** would not just pluck its ideas out of the sky, but would use ideas and influences which it thought could click with its target market – sophisticated teenagers to twenty-somethings. As with many campaigns of the past, it would probably be influenced by the works of well-known artists, and styles used in other media. But whatever it chooses, the creative team has to get the approval of the client company first.

Tempting trends

Most campaigns are influenced by artistic and media trends of both past and present, depending on the nature of the product and the target market. Part of the imaginary jeans' campaign is very much in the present, reflecting the new **line** with its special pocket for the mobile phone. This is an essential approach for any product that has seemed rather stale and old. Trying to keep in touch with its young market, the campaign might have been influenced by a movie, in this case, probably *The Beach*. As part of the product's sophisticated image, and bearing in mind the twenty-somethings market, the campaign might also reflect, for example, the stylish beach garden with its grasses and pebbles, designed by the late film-maker Derek Jarman.

The agency would test these ideas, probably in **storyboard** form, on several **focus groups**: teenagers, twenty-something professionals, and people in their forties. They would probably be trying to attract the first two groups, but might have some tussles with their client, who would not wish to alienate the older group from its entire range!

Governments can also influence advertising. In the mid 1960s, British trade was promoted by Prime Minister Harold Wilson with the slogan 'Buy British'. You can see this theme reflected in clothing sold here in London's Carnaby Street during the same era. In the late 1990s, the UK was dubbed 'Cool Britannia'.

Going pop

The arts and advertising have always had a close relationship. Pop music and its videos, fashion, films and art trends have all been used, copied or even made fun of in advertisements and **commercials**. This 'borrowing' helps the advertiser to relate to its target market, and attract it. The influence has also worked the other way round. One of the most famous modern artists, the late Andy Warhol, used repeat patterns of mass-produced products to create works of art in the 1950s and 1960s. These are thought to have been the artist's comment on the greed and lack of individuality of **consumerism**, and on advertising itself. In 1999, McDonald's copied Warhol's bright repeat patterns to advertise its burgers.

An international event can make countries very fashionable in the advertising world. Australia has become even more popular since the 2000 Sydney Olympics. Advertising for the Games, and the nation as a whole, used the symbol of the striking Opera House to give the nation a forward-thinking, city image.

A cool country

From the late 1990s, Australia has been seen as a trendy place. But advertisers for its products have often used the old, **stereotypical** humorous and macho male image to attract an audience. Advertising in other countries has jumped on the bandwagon and 'borrowed' Australia to help sell products! In 2000, McDonald's created a radio commercial for the UK read by an Australian, and with the copy, 'the burger with cheese and outback sauce'.

Producing the Goods

Paper power

With the concepts developed, tested and approved, the jeans' **campaign** is now ready to go to different media production companies to make the advertisements and **commercials**. One of these will produce printed advertisements. These are **hoardings**, posters and flyers, which compete with newspapers and television for a large slice of advertising sales.

Pasting it up

Advertising on hoardings is unmissable. For big **brand** names, the image and **slogan** used on the hoarding are often compatible with those used in the product's TV commercial, which reinforces its message. Hoardings are printed in strips, which are carefully pasted together on billboards. They are changed regularly. Many modern billboards are built in sections that revolve automatically in time with each other, enabling more than one advertisement to be displayed at once. Others are designed to scroll up and down. Lights illuminate some billboards at night, giving 24-hour coverage.

Posting it up

Posters advertising products are usually pinned up in retail outlets, using similar images and slogans to hoardings but on a smaller scale. This could be helpful to a jeans' campaign, where several makes of jean might be folded on shelves, all looking rather similar. A poster advertising the new range should encourage customers to buy the brand. But it must make the new **line** look special, or will it just promote all the jeans in the shop!

Repeating the message

One of the biggest problems for any multimedia advertising campaign is co-ordinating images and slogans. A hoarding, poster or flyer is more effective if it reminds the consumer of the central image in the TV commercial, and the repeated **endline** in the radio commercial. Technically, one of the greatest problems is maintaining constant colours on the **visuals** – the blue of the jeans must be the same for printed as well as moving media.

On the job
A designer creating a hoarding for a client must understand the product being advertised and the market at which it is being pitched. The designer also has to be able to represent the concept of the advertisement in a simple, clear way. It must make an instant impact without small print that cannot be seen from a distance.

Flying high

Flyers distributed in the streets are often handed out at random. They use the basic message, image and **copy** created for larger newspaper and magazine advertisements on the front of the flyer, but enable people to read more detailed information on the back. Flyers posted through doors carefully target people within a particular income bracket, which is often tied to the areas in which people live. A flyer campaign is carried out over a certain period. Both of these strategies enable the advertiser to work out whether the fliers have had any real impact on sales. This very specific marketing has meant that flyers are often as successful as television in persuading people to part with their money – in translating advertising into actual purchases.

The cost-effectiveness of using flyers is huge, as printing costs are cheap. Many flyers are created on computer software and run off on computer printers. This modern technology has allowed very small businesses to promote their products at a reasonable cost and enables changes to be made to advertisements very quickly and cheaply.

For the 'dream jeanzzz' campaign, flyers could be distributed by, say, a music store – sales assistants adding a flyer to the customer's purchase bag. It could also be inserted into selected newspapers or magazines. In these ways, the flyer could target its youth market.

Sign painting is a time-consuming job, so sign painters are employed where goods and services will not change for a long time. These are very basic advertisements, informing and reminding rather than trying to surprise or create a deep interest. A sign painter is reinforcing the effect of the neon sign by painting the shop's façade.

The press accounts for over half of all advertising, so a **media planner** for a jeans' **campaign** would see advertising in newspapers and magazines as central to its aims. Advertisements in national newspapers can be targeted according to social group and income, while local newspapers have a very large readership, which local businesses take full advantage of.

Getting it on the page

A high-profile jeans' campaign for a new line would need **display advertisements** for national and possibly regional newspapers. These are the large advertisements often seen on the inside pages of the papers themselves and in colour supplements. The media buyer would liaise with the advertising manager of the newspaper to secure advertising space for specific pages and issues of the paper.

Extra special

Special lifestyle sections of national dailies, and colour supplements of weekend newspapers, are perfect for advertising a new **line** of jeans. Many articles written for these pages by consumer journalists are not direct advertisements for a particular **brand**. But the advertiser and the newspaper's advertising manager can arrange for a jeans' advertisement to be placed close to an article that would be relevant to it.

The right design

The advertiser's design team might want the same photographed image to be used in colour for a supplement, and black and white for a newspaper display advertisement. Although colour prints and transparencies can be printed in black and white, they tend to lose their contrast and sharpness, so the photographer shoots separate colour and black-and-white film.

Oxfam
KOSOVO
Crisis Appeal

"These people have been through hell. How much more can they endure?"

Chris Stalker, Oxfam
Former Yugoslav Republic of Macedonia
April 1999

Right now, in the crammed border camps of Albania and Macedonia, Oxfam is protecting tens of thousands of Kosovo refugees from a new danger: deadly disease from filthy, infected drinking water.

You can help. We're already providing over 120,000 people with clean, life-saving water, and many with warm clothes and shelter.

But the flood of refugees continues. We can do so much more, and you can help. **Just £25 from you can sterilise enough drinking water for 80 people.** And Oxfam will be there in the future, helping families in the region to rebuild shattered lives.

Please send your gift to
Oxfam Kosovo Crisis Appeal
using the coupon below or phone on
01865 313131
You can also donate via our website: www.oxfam.org.uk

Yes, I want to help. Here is my gift of:
£25 ☐   £50 ☐   £100 ☐   £250 ☐   £_____
Mr, Mrs, Miss, Ms
Address

Postcode
Please send to: Oxfam, Room BB06, Freepost, Oxford OX2 7BR

Ⓧ **Oxfam**

Oxfam GB is a member of Oxfam International
Registered charity no 202918

Most companies do not want their product advertised next to bad news. However, national newspapers often advertise international charities on the front or inside pages, especially during a special appeal, such as a famine or war. Aid organizations include methods of donating money at the bottom of the advertisement.

A newspaper designer knows the dimensions and positions of display ads before the **copy** of the news items has been finished. This means that they can be **blocked out**, and the newspaper articles fitted in around them. It also means that a media planner knows roughly the size, shape and position of display ads for each newspaper, and can target the one that best meets the needs of the campaign.

The composition of the picture – the way each visual element in it is arranged – is very important. But the image can be cut, or cropped, and digitally manipulated to perfect the composition.

On the job

A fashion and still-life photographer needs very good technical skills. He or she must also have a keen eye for composition (how the subjects in the picture are arranged) and interesting angles – something that is partly instinctive and partly practice. The photographer must understand the aims of the client, but be original at the same time. A relationship of trust with the model used for fashion advertisements is essential.

Seen on screen

Over 95 per cent of households in richer nations own a television set, so advertising on television offers the **media planner** huge coverage. It also enables the creative team to get the message across using movement, sound, colour and graphics. Cinema has a smaller audience, but the enormous screen certainly packs a punch! Big screen **commercials**, though, do not always advertise big companies. Small local services, such as restaurants, take advantage of the local audience's needs.

The choice of location is one of the most important factors in creating the correct mood for the product. Here, a beach in Kenya is being used for a St Ivel Gold margarine commercial.

Precious seconds

Some TV commercials are short, 10 to 20-second slots which show the product and its uses clearly and simply. The product and its qualities are reinforced at the end with a repetition of the **brand** name and the **slogan**, known in this medium as an **endline**. Other commmercials are between 30 and 60 seconds of dramatized advertising – playing out a story or theme that is intriguing or attractive enough on its own to engage the audience. Sometimes it is only at the end that those watching know what is being advertised.

A media planner will choose the length and complexity of commercial according to his or her budget. Longer commercials shot in an expensive location or using lots of special effects can cost several hundred thousand pounds to produce.

The big screen

Movies shown in cinemas draw a captive, specific audience, which advertisers are keen to target. Each screened commercial is given its own certificate to show its suitability for showing with a particular film. SAWA – the Screen Advertising World Association – is the US-based trade association that promotes cinema commercials.

Producing the goods

For a short commercial on, for example, a local cable network, the advertiser can ask the television company itself to create a commercial for it, costing just a few hundred pounds. All TV stations have the facilities to screen a still picture of the product and provide a voice-over for it – an unseen actor's voice reinforcing the product's name and essential qualities. But for a longer expensive commercial on a major channel the media planner will nearly always engage an advertising agency. The agency puts together proposals together with **storyboards** or animatics. These are sketches shot on video to give an idea of movement and mood. Once the idea and script has been chosen by the client, it is shown to an advertising standards authority (an advertising **watchdog**) for approval, and then a production team and director are hired – or a whole production company. Before it is shown, the commercial has to be seen by the standards authority again (see page 42).

Shop as you watch

The jeans' **campaign** could include buying a slot on a shopping channel, where the qualities of the jeans could be demonstrated thoroughly. But a media planner might feel that the relaxed, but cool, image of the product would be lost by this method. Penetration (how well the medium reaches its audience), though, is good, as each product is given repeated, lengthy and detailed coverage throughout the day.

One of the sales' gimmicks used on shopping channels is to persuade the viewer that they will never get another chance to buy a particular exclusive product – or to buy it as cheaply. This is a good strategy for a company that does not see the product as part of a long-term range – just a one-off. It is also a clever way of getting rid of old stock! But it would not be a successful gimmick for a jeans' company wanting to advertise its new **line** as part of a developing range.

Technical tips

The media planner studies appropriate programme **ratings** to see if advertising close to them would be worth it. He or she consults ratings companies, who, through telephone questionnaires and other methods, work out the TVR, or Television Ratings. From these, the media planner can find out the coverage of particular programmes (the percentage of people who could be watching) and then work out the frequency at which the commercial should be shown around or between these programmes for maximum effect.

What's the story?

The advertising agency thought of a storyline for the 'dream jeanzzz' **campaign**. For future **lines** in the range it might consider a mini-series based on the original characters on the beach. This and other techniques are used in TV **commercials** to keep the audience interested in a product or company.

Getting to you

Creators and directors for commercials use many methods to persuade us to buy a product. These include humour, and encouraging us to identify with the users of the product on screen. Sometimes the characters are the kinds of people we would like to be rather than actually are. They are funnier, smarter, more stylish and so on. We want to be like them, so we buy the product – well, that is the theory, anyway!

Certain family sitcom or TV soap-style commercials advertising domestic products, such as stock cubes and washing powder, have run for years. They are designed to give the viewer a feeling of security and cosiness. This would not be suitable for the jeans' campaign, which relies on independence as part of its appeal.

True stories

Charities and international aid organizations use television commercials to highlight problems and attract donations using real and often gruesome human interest stories. Some of these commercials have been criticized for showing developing countries in a helpless, hopeless light when in fact 'self-help' is the aim of most of these nations.

Animals are a favourite subject for commercials. Hedgehogs have been used to advertise a car's superior brakes and chimpanzees have starred in a long-running campaign for tea.

On the job
Acting for commercials requires short bursts of deep concentration and near-perfection every time. The actor has to be very patient, as the director can do many takes to get the right effect. The actor and writer Griff Rhys Jones said that working on a series of commercials for Holsten Pils Lager was 'Ten times longer than anything else I've ever done.' Another actor had to bite into 40 Cadbury's Flakes before she got it right!

The art of suggestion

Advertisers try to suggest what a product could make us feel or even become. Colour, lighting, background, movement and so on create moods and suggestions – of season, temperature, age, seriousness and so on. These act like a trigger. We begin to associate all these elements with feelings – of happiness, love, hope, security and so on. We begin to imagine ourselves in the screened situation, using the same product. Suggestion, too, can be found in music and sound. It is used in many TV commercials as a substitute for dialogue and helps the viewer to understand the product's appeal.

The director is responsible for the effect of the finished commercial. Many movie directors began in TV commercials, such as the UK's Tony Scott. His brother, Ridley, made movies first, but has directed commercials since! A well-directed TV commercial is highly respected in the film world.

Famous film actors are paid enormous sums of money to appear in TV commercials. In 2000, years after his last appearance in a James Bond movie, Roger Moore played out humorous, Bond-like scenes to advertise a credit card. But do we take more notice of 'Bond' than the product? Post-campaign research can give advertisers the answer.

On the web

These days, a high-profile advertising **campaign** for jeans would almost certainly include the Internet. From small banner ads at the corner of web pages to shopping sites, the Internet can provide a service for most aims and budgets. The jeans' company might see setting up its own on-line shopping site as a long-term **investment**, using it to promote and sell other products if 'dream jeanzzz' proved successful.

Brave new world

The Internet is changing the way that advertising is being conceived and created, and has given a different slant on marketing. Its wide access means that advertisers are less able to target a particular culture or nation, so their creative teams have to design with a range of tastes and traditions in mind, or allow a powerful culture, such as that of the USA, to dominate. Many advertisers, though, target age ranges. As a result, a globalized youth culture is being created – its members encouraged through advertising to own particular goods or use certain services as part of a youth identity. The **marketing manager** of the new **line** in jeans would need to get onto the Internet in order to attract this client group.

Making it matter

Banner advertisements in the corners of website pages are very small and need to attract the viewer's attention. Designers use splashes of bright primary colours, bold lettering and clear logos, which enable the viewer, flicking through the web pages, to know instantly what is being advertised. Some banners are designed to flash or move about, making them easier to spot, although this can be rather irritating!

Often, the banner ad is related to the topic of the website page it is sited on, but not always. For the jeans' campaign, it could be tied to pop music, extreme sports, TV and chat sites, and others that are surfed by young people.

Buying on-line

A jeans' company could also create its own on-line shopping site, as have countless well-known sportswear brands, such as Nike. But there are downsides to on-line shopping, especially for clothes. As with television and catalogue shopping, choosing the right size and shape of garment can be a problem, and goods often have to be returned. But the advantage over television shopping channels is that you can access the site for the goods you want, whenever you want – as long as you can be connected easily!

Money matters

The success of shopping websites has led to many purchases being made over the Internet. But payment is nearly always by credit card and there is increasing concern at the lack of security. Who should be responsible for the security of our money on the Internet – the Internet server, the website owner or the customer's credit card company? This remains a burning issue today.

Finding the site

A campaign manager for a new design of jeans would want to use an efficient Internet search engine, or 'browser', so that people could access the site easily. Search engines, such as Google, are well-known and advertise their own services using other media, such as television.

Choosing the registered name of the website is crucial, and should be original. Some names are amusing or interesting but do not instantly tell you what is on offer. 'dreamjeanzzz.com', created from the name of the new line, would be a reasonable name to choose for the jeans' campaign. Good website names are very valuable. Some individuals have registered **brand** names and then sold them to the actual brand name companies for a lot of money.

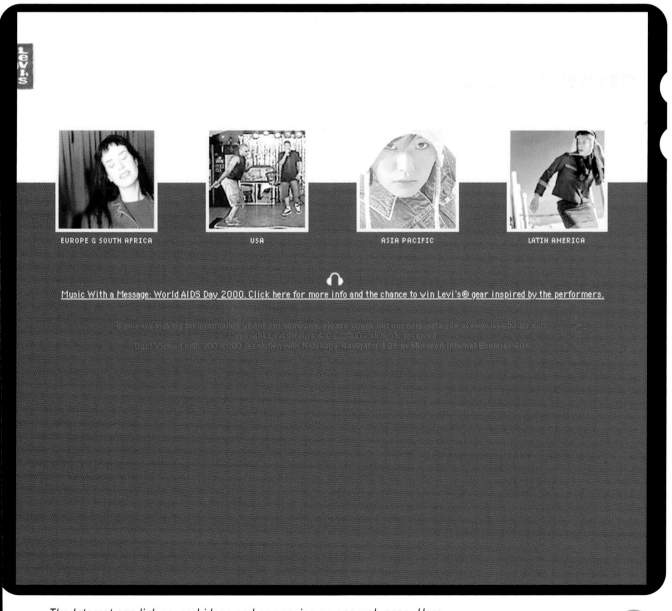

EUROPE & SOUTH AFRICA   USA   ASIA PACIFIC   LATIN AMERICA

Music With a Message: World AIDS Day 2000. Click here for more info and the chance to win Levi's® gear inspired by the performers.

The Internet can link several ideas and companies on one web page. Here, Levi.com is linked with musicians from diverse regions of the world through the promotion of World AIDS Day.

Invisible ads

Radio **commercials** persuade us to buy a product or service using the human voice, music, sound effects and clever **copy**. The **media planner** for a jeans' **campaign** might use a radio commercial to suggest the soft, smooth feel of the fabric, and the 'dreamy' mood.

Why radio?

With satellites relaying radio signals long distances, and with the use of the Internet, radio is now a medium with very wide coverage. In spite of this, making radio commercials has remained relatively cheap. This is partly because production costs are less than those for other media, such as television.

Hearing is believing

Radio commercials can last from ten seconds to a minute, and cost from a few hundred pounds to several thousand. Simple, cheap commercials using pre-recorded sound effects, jingles and a voice-over by a freelance presenter or jobbing actor, rather than a celebrity, are often made in local or regional radio stations. Longer, expensive commercials are created by production companies. These are employed by advertising agencies for their clients.

Effective commercials can be made using a variety of techniques to grab and hold our attention. Everything from humour to explosions of strange noises help to engage the listener. Jingles – short passages of music that represent the product and what it stands for – remind the listener of the product when they hear the jingle again, perhaps on television as well as radio. But one of the most important features is the **endline**, which tells you the name of the product or service in the dying seconds of the commercial. The endline is rather like a punchline in a joke, and is often repeated up to half a dozen times to reinforce the product and the message.

In the studio

The new jeans' radio commercial would probably be between 20 and 30 seconds long, and would be written as quite a complex mini-play recorded in a live acting studio, with many sounds and effects. The recording studio is well equipped to produce these. It has hard screens to reflect sounds, making them 'live' or 'bright'. Soft, cloth-covered screens absorb sound, creating a 'dead' tone. For a damped-down, outdoor effect, the studio walls are padded. Different sections of floor surface and a set of stairs enable actors and studio assistants to make realistic movement sounds. The surfaces include carpet, wood, concrete and stone. Doors, drawers, cupboards and curtains are set on wheels, to be placed in front of the correct microphone as they are opened or closed.

Technical tips

Regular actors for radio commercials have studios set up in their own homes. They link with the radio's studio control room directly through special phone lines (Integrated Services Digital Network – or ISDN), or make pre-recorded tapes which are then mixed with sound effects and music.

Delivering the lines

Many actors are employed for their 'safe' delivery of a radio commercial's lines using a soft tone and a low note. This is known as a 'brown' voice, and belongs mainly to older men. This type of voice often advertises products that we want to feel secure about, such as **insurance policies** and medicines. The listener only hears the actor, but the actor often uses facial expressions and hand gestures while recording. This helps them get to grips with the character they are playing. The jeans' campaign would want to use a younger, fresher, but relaxed voice.

In sound booths, like this one, actors are often given several scripts for different commercials to reel off in just one session.

On the job

A writer for radio commercials needs to understand the qualities of the product being advertised, the target audience, the aims of the client and the client's overall campaign. He or she needs to be able to write to very strict time limits, and use every second to good effect. Humour, a knack for punchy endlines and an understanding of the impact of different sound effects are important.

Pushing the Message

Selling space

The media buyer for a jeans' **campaign** has to decide which type of media will promote the product best and provide good value for money. Media sales staff then buy advertising space in newspapers or on the Internet, and **commercial** slots on radio or television.

The right time

The commercial slots sold during popular programmes, such as the sitcom 'Frasier', are usually for glamorous and trendy items, such as cars, make-up or luxury items, to reflect people's perception of the actors and characters in the sitcom. The advertiser hopes to appeal to the viewers' desire to be like the stars they are watching.

The cost of buying a commercial slot on radio and television depends on the length of the commercial and the time during which it will be broadcast. Prime-time radio slots are expensive as they coincide with what is known as 'drive time' – when people are getting ready for work or school, and travelling, listening to the radio as they go. This is when radio gets its best **ratings** and so is valuable to the advertiser. Prime time lasts from about 6.00 a.m. to 9.30 a.m., and then from about 4.30 p.m. to 6.30 p.m. During these periods, a short commercial of about 10 or 20 seconds can cost several times more than at other times of the day, when the same length will cost only a few hundred pounds. The advertiser's media buyer will purchase a **package** from the radio station. This is a deal which will guarantee that the commercial is scheduled for slots in certain programmes, and repeated a set number of times.

Prime-time television is generally in the evening, from about 7.30 p.m. until 10.00 p.m. The cost of a commercial slot during these times, or coinciding with very popular programmes, such as sitcoms or an international sporting activity, can cost several hundred thousands of pounds. If another advertiser offers a higher price for a slot, then the first advertiser is pushed out!

The right place

Newspaper sections attract advertising that is relevant to the topics that they specialize in. A tele-ad salesforce is employed to sell the spaces allotted for each of these sections over the telephone, while around the country, advertising representatives (reps) draw in advertising from businesses located within a specified area.

Tele-salespeople use a Rate Card to tell their customers how much their advertisement will cost. **Display ads** are usually charged by the amount of space they take up, while **classified ads** are paid for by the number of words printed plus any extra design features, such as bold box lines or a decorative border. There are often special offers for first-time display ad buyers.

The right page

Internet search engines are good places to advertise products, as they are so widely used. An advertiser has to pay the search engine every time its advertisement is accessed, or 'hit', to give the user more information about the product. A small counter at the corner of the engine's pages notches up the number of people using each site, so it is easy to calculate how much the advertiser has to pay.

A national broadsheet newspaper (a large, more 'serious' newspaper) employs dozens of tele-ad salespeople who work in shifts. To do their job effectively they need a friendly but businesslike telephone manner, a clear speaking voice, an instant knowledge of the services they can provide and a lot of patience.

Manipulation

Television and radio commercials interrupt programming, and some critics accuse them of manipulating vulnerable people, especially children and the poor. For these reasons, broadcasting stations in The Netherlands are not permitted to sell commercial slots.

Putting it all together

The jeans' advertising **campaign** concentrated mainly on mainstream media. But there are other elements to an intra-media advertising policy (one which uses several media) that are not strictly classed as advertising. Some are fine details that help to promote the product or the company.

A good display

Attractive presentation is a good selling point, and the shop window in particular is an important promotional opportunity for a product. However, a **brand** of jeans without its own store usually has no say in what will be displayed in someone else's store. A **media planner** for a brand of jeans might negotiate with a retail chain to show its new **line** for a certain length of time. It could give each store posters and flyers to supplement the window dressing.

Inside retail outlets, jeans are generally displayed folded on shelves or hung on racks. There is often nothing to distinguish one brand from another. A creative team might consider making its own display rack for each store, perhaps with a jeans' poster pinned above it to draw the shoppers.

Carrying a shopping bag produced by luxury stores gives the carrier status and triggers a reminder of the store when other people see it. These bags often do not change in colour and style for many years.

Wrapping it up

Packaging is promotion – and well-designed packaging can encourage a buyer to choose a particular brand over another, especially if the item is intended as a gift. The creative team that designs posters, **hoardings** and newspaper advertisements, and which co-ordinates the look of the product through visual image, colour and logo usually designs the packaging as well. Clothing companies have generally been slow to pick up on the value of packaging.

Something extra

Samples, give-aways and scratchcards are often used to promote a new product, especially foods and cosmetics. Breakfast cereals are well-known for their plastic toy gifts and cardboard cut-out projects on the backs of the packets. The jeans' campaign might negotiate with a music store to give away a CD token with every pair of the new line sold. But the promotion would be given a time limit.

Consumer groups often criticize the practice of offering give-aways, competitions, scratchcards and so on with a product. They are concerned that these are just gimmicks that disguise the quality and real value of the product being bought and are a poor substitute for straightforward information about it.

Attention to detail in the packaging of luxury goods, like these chocolates, increases the item's potential as a gift or as a purchase on special occasions, such as Valentine's Day.

On the job

A window dresser's job is like designing sets for a production at the theatre. He or she has to know what will catch the window-shopper's eye, so has to be up-to-date with trends. An awareness of the image of the shop and the brands being sold in it is also important. For clothes, the window dresser has to know the season's colours and themes.

Under the Microscope

Is it right? Is it fair?

Was the jeans' **campaign** honest? Was each advertisement or **commercial** fair? Do the jeans themselves live up to their **hype**? Advertising **watchdogs** and public pressure groups try to make sure that we are not subjected to tasteless presentation and false claims.

Checking it out

Before an advertisement or commercial is displayed or broadcast, advertisers' and agents' legal departments check that all the necessary rights have been bought for broadcasting music or using images belonging to other companies. The advertisement also has to abide by regulations controlling decency and taste. These are monitored by government or independent organizations. In the UK, the main body is the Advertising Standards Authority, in Australia, the Australian Advertising Standards Council, and in the USA, the American Advertising Federation. There are often separate organizations for radio and television. In the UK, the Independent Television Commission (ITC), like many other monitoring organizations, advertises its own service. Promising to make sure that each advertiser abides by codes of conduct expected by most viewers, it uses the **slogan** 'We will ITC that it does'.

Deciding what's right

Each country has different ideas about what is acceptable and what is not. In parts of continental Europe, for instance, nudity on **hoardings** is allowed, whereas in the UK and Australia, it is not. Many nations encourage advertising of condoms as they prevent unwanted pregnancies, disease and AIDS, but in the UK and some countries with religious objections to condoms, this combination of commercial advertising and health promotion is not allowed. Strobe lighting on television has had to be controlled, as it is thought to trigger migraines and epileptic fits. The possibility of flashing an advertising image in the middle of a television programme to influence the viewer, targeting them without their knowledge, is seen as unfair. This 'subliminal' messaging, although banned in most countries, is becoming a theory discredited by some scientists.

Ultimately, viewers and the listeners will decide what is a tasteful and morally acceptable advertisement. If they are repelled by them, they will often not buy the products or services.

Gender and race

Advertisements are continually being criticized for race and gender **stereotyping**. In many countries, minority groups are not represented enough, or are not shown in a wide variety of situations. Women are still often portrayed as useless at anything practical, such as DIY or car repairs, and men as macho tough guys who cannot cope with cooking or cleaning.

Is it the truth?

Trading standards organizations make sure that the benefits advertised for each product are true. Again, what an advertiser can claim differs from country to country. In the USA, for example, advertisements for face creams have not been able to claim anti-ageing properties, whereas in the UK, regulations are only just coming into force on this issue.

Making the most of it

Films and well-known television programmes such as 'The Simpsons' promote themselves through many types of media, from articles in media magazines, through hoardings to **merchandising**. This is aimed at young people and is sometimes seen as exploitative. Television targets children aggressively with commercials, especially before major festivals, such as Christmas. But in many countries, commercials for a particular product are not allowed to be broadcast close to TV programmes that are directly related to that product. Nor are the advertisers allowed to suggest that children will be left out and shunned by their friends if they do not have the latest clothing or toy.

UNITED COLORS OF BENETTON.

United Colours of Benetton have often been criticized for advertising stark images on hoardings, such as a man dying of AIDS. But some people feel that their advertising campaigns reflect the world as it really is, not the usual dream-world pushed by advertisers.

The verdict – the future

The jeans' advertiser will not know how effective the advertising **campaign** has been until sales figures for the product start rolling in. Even then it is difficult to know exactly whether or not advertising was responsible for success – or failure! The campaign used all the available media that it could afford. But future developments will provide a still faster, broader range of advertising.

A question of access

After reading this book, you might look a little differently at the advertisements you see around you. You might be more suspicious of the motives behind them, but also more appreciative of the thought and artistry that goes into them. While you are thinking about these things, advertisers are beavering away at their desks, trying to find better and faster ways of attracting your attention – of entertaining you and of making you part with your money.

In the future, many more of us will have access to Internet advertising. Computer miniaturization in the form of WAPS is already letting us carry advertising around with us and access it day or night. There are on-line shopping channels 24 hours a day. On a larger scale, **hoardings** might become advertising film screens, like those huge replay screens at sports' grounds.

But rather than creating new types of advertising media, the immediate future will probably bring speedier access to it. New computer software will make accessing Internet sites even quicker, enabling the user to scan an even greater number of advertising sites within a short space of time. This will mean that advertisers have to use even better ways of grabbing our attention so that we do not miss the message as our eyes flick across the screen.

WAPS have advantages for advertisers – and drawbacks. They allow advertising through telephone and e-mail messaging, and the Internet. Some WAPS even have a separate radio system, so the listener can hear commercials. But some people find using three buttons per letter very time-consuming for sending e-mails and accessing the Internet. Voice recognition for WAPS is perhaps a solution for the future.

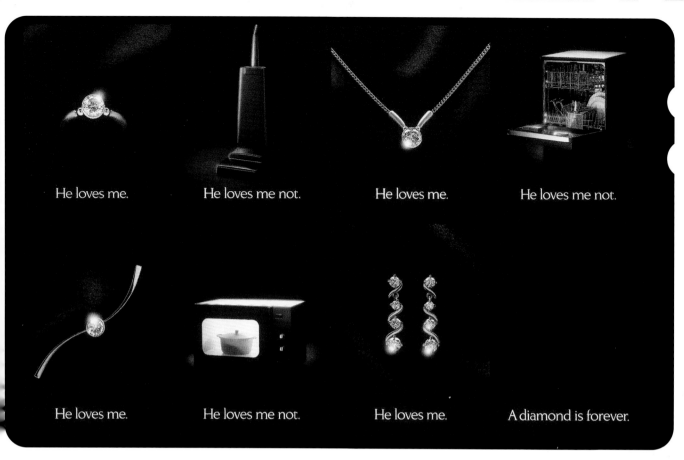

He loves me.   He loves me not.   He loves me.   He loves me not.

He loves me.   He loves me not.   He loves me.   A diamond is forever.

*National and international advertising awards show appreciation for all those involved in the advertising industry. On 12 July 2000 'A diamond is forever,' was voted the number one **endline** of the 20th century. The slogan is clever – diamonds are the hardest gem of all and therefore will 'last forever', as will love (or so the advertisers are hinting!). A diamond ring symbolizes both of these things.*

Issues for the future

As global advertising increases, so do many of the issues surrounding it. Are ads for the many or the few? For the rich only? Do adverts unite or divide society? Do they promote envy and greed – and theft? Do they exclude people, for example the disabled? Do they encourage categorization?

Technical tips

Internet services accessible on TV screens using a cordless keyboard are an advertisers' dream. The Internet can be used without a computer or WAP, and the viewer is be able to link ordinary television broadcasts to relevant websites. It is predicted by the TV company ONdigital that by 2005, a third of all on-line shopping sales will be made via this television facility. In 2000 the company spent £8 million on advertising the concept.

Glossary

account a particular advertising campaign for an advertising agency's client

account executive someone who works for an advertising agency, liaising between the agency's creative team and the client or the client's marketing manager

blocked out spaces left for advertisements on a newspaper or magazine layout

brand trademark or trade name

campaign an advertising strategy for a particular product, using different media

catchword an easily remembered name or word that the viewer or listener will associate with a product

classified ad an advertisement placed in a particular category of a newspaper's advertisement section, such as cars

client base the people who could use a particular product and who might be attracted into buying it

commercial an advertisement created for television, cinema or radio

communist a type of government, such as that in China, in which representitives are not selected in a multi-party system, and in which wealth is supposed to be shared

consumerism an appetite for buying goods

copy written text, advertising slogans, endlincs and catchphrases

copywriter someone who writes copy

direct mailing sending advertisements through the letterbox, mobile phone or e-mail

display advertisement the large newspaper advertisements placed throughout the paper or its supplements – also used to describe magazine advertisements

endline a repeated slogan used especially in radio to reinforce the message of the product and the brand in the listener's mind

ethical morally right; something that does not harm people

focus group a group of people from a similar age group and with similar lifestyles who are asked specific questions as part of market research

font typeface or style of lettering

hoarding large outdoor advertising board

hype promoting and praising a product probably more than it deserves

insurance policy paying to make sure that the costs of accidents, fire, ill-health and so on will be covered if these things happen to you

investment putting money into something in order to get even more money back in the end

layout   the plan and design of a printed advertisement set out on paper or on a computer screen

line   a particular style of product within a range of styles, or a particular product within a set of similar products made by the same company

marketing manager   a company's advertising and promotions co-ordinator who also employs the advertising agencies for each project

market research   finding out what people's habits, likes and dislikes are, so that an advertising campaign can target its market effectively – also used to find out what that market is

market saturation   when a company has made so many sales within a particular area or from a group of people that it can realistically make no more

market share   the percentage of sales a company makes for a particular product in competition with other companies for the same product

media planner   someone who plans which media are to be used for a particular advertising campaign

merchandising   promoting a film, TV programme and so on by creating and selling goods associated with it

package   an agreement struck between the client or their advertiser and a broadcasting company to transmit a commercial a certain number of times within a particular period

rating   the size of an audience watching or listening to a particular programme on television or radio

return on investment   the amount of money a company gets back from advertising through sales – a negative return on investment means that the advertising has failed to increase profits

slogan   a snappy phrase that will help the viewer or listener instantly recall the product in their mind

sole trader   a company run and worked by one person

stereotyping   giving a false or narrow impression of a group of people

still   a picture taken from a moving TV or cinema film, used for promotional purposes

storyboard   a set of drawn sketches showing the theme and storyline of an advertising campaign

trade fair   a huge market place in which companies display, demonstrate and advertise their goods to other companies within their own industry

visuals   advertising media that you can see

watchdog   an organization that monitors moral and legal standards in the advertising media

Index

Titles in the *Behind Media* series include:

Hardback   0 431 11450 1

Hardback   0 431 11452 8

Hardback   0 431 11463 3

Hardback   0 431 11461 7

Hardback   0 431 11460 9

Hardback   0 431 11462 5

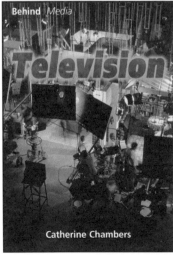

Hardback   0 431 11451 X

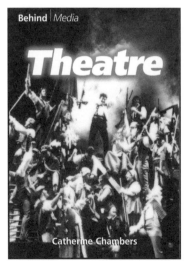

Hardback   0 431 11453 6

Find out about other Heinemann books on our website www.heinemann.co.uk/library